The DeepSeek R1 Revolution: How a New AI is Redefining the Future of Intelligence

Breaking Down the Technology Behind China's Most Advanced AI Model

Owen Delaney

COPYRIGHT

DISCLAIMER

This book is for informational and educational purposes only. While every effort has been made to ensure accuracy, the author and publisher make no guarantees regarding completeness or applicability. Readers should conduct their own research and seek professional advice before making decisions based on this content.

The views expressed are those of the author and do not reflect any company or organization. References to specific technologies or entities do not imply endorsement. AI is a rapidly evolving field, and some information may become outdated. The author and publisher are not liable for any consequences arising from the use of this book.

All trademarks, product names, and company names mentioned in this book remain the property of their respective owners. Their inclusion is purely for reference and does not imply any association, sponsorship, or endorsement.

Table Of Contents

Owen Delaney.. 0

COPYRIGHT...1

DISCLAIMER..2

Table Of Contents... 4

Introduction..7

Chapter 1.. 15

The Birth of DeepSeek R1.................................. 15

    Who Developed DeepSeek R1?...................... 15

    The Research Team and Their Vision............. 16

    How DeepSeek R1 Compares to Previous AI
    Models...18

The AI Arms Race: How China is Positioning
Itself in AI Development...................................... 19

Chapter 2.. 22

Understanding DeepSeek R1's Core Capabilities
22

    What Sets DeepSeek R1 Apart?.....................23

    Its Performance in Reasoning, Coding, and
    Problem-Solving...26

    Benchmarks Against OpenAI's Models...........29

    Early Tests and Real-World Applications........ 31

Chapter 3.. 33

Chain of Thought Reasoning – How DeepSeek
R1 Thinks...33

    What is Chain of Thought (CoT) reasoning?.. 35

    How DeepSeek R1 applies step-by-step logic 36

Examples of CoT in action (math, coding, decision-making)...38

The impact of structured reasoning in AI performance...40

Chapter 4... **42**

Reinforcement Learning – How DeepSeek R1 Learns on Its Own...................................42

What makes DeepSeek R1 different from traditional AI training?...................................... 44

The role of reinforcement learning in AI development...46

Comparing DeepSeek R1's learning process to human.. 48

How trial and error improves AI decision-making 50

Chapter 6... **53**

Policy Optimization – The Science Behind Stability.. **53**

The Mathematical Foundation of DeepSeek R1's Training.. 55

How Stability is Maintained During Learning.. 57

Techniques like Clipping and K Divergence Explained... 59

Why Policy Optimization Matters in AI Development.. 61

Chapter 7... **64**

Model Distillation – Making DeepSeek R1 Accessible.. **64**

Why DeepSeek R1's 671 Billion Parameters Are a Challenge.. 66

How Smaller Distilled Models (e.g., 7B) Replicate Its Capabilities.................................68

The Surprising Performance of Distilled Models vs. GPT-4.. 71

Chapter 8.. 74

Real-World Applications and Future Possibilities...74

Ethical Considerations of AI with Self-Learning Capabilities.......................................78

The Future of AI Competition: OpenAI, DeepSeek, and Beyond................................ 81

What the Development of DeepSeek R1 Means for AI Accessibility... 83

Conclusion.. 86

Introduction

The world is on the brink of an intelligence revolution, one that is unfolding not in the pages of science fiction but in the rapidly advancing corridors of artificial intelligence. From the moment humankind imagined machines that could think, reason, and evolve on their own, we have been racing toward a future where AI is no longer just a tool but a force shaping our reality.

That future is no longer distant. It is here. And at the heart of this seismic shift stands DeepSeek R1—an AI model that is not only redefining what machines are capable of but also ceventuallyhallenging the very foundations of artificial intelligence itself.

Artificial intelligence has always been about pushing boundaries, about teaching machines to think, to solve problems, to assist, and to innovate. We have witnessed the rise of

OpenAI's models, Google's deep learning advancements, and countless breakthroughs that have propelled AI into nearly every facet of human life. But DeepSeek R1 is different. It is not just another AI model in the lineup. It represents something more—a profound shift in how AI learns, reasons, and surpasses expectations.

Developed by a cutting-edge research team in China, DeepSeek R1 has emerged as a formidable competitor in the AI arms race, standing toe-to-toe with some of the most advanced models in the world. Yet, its significance extends far beyond simple comparisons. What makes DeepSeek R1 so groundbreaking is its ability to engage in sophisticated reasoning, problem-solving, and adaptation—qualities that have long been the holy grail of artificial intelligence.

At its core, DeepSeek R1 embodies the next evolution of machine intelligence, integrating a unique reinforcement learning process that allows it to teach itself, much like a human learns from experience. It doesn't just execute tasks; it understands them. It doesn't merely generate responses; it refines them through self-reflection and correction. And perhaps most impressively, it demonstrates a capacity for what researchers call "Chain of Thought" reasoning—a method that enables AI to break down complex problems, analyze them step by step, and arrive at conclusions with an almost eerie sense of logic.

Imagine a machine capable of solving intricate mathematical equations, writing flawless code, or engaging in deep philosophical debates—not by brute force, but by truly understanding the process. DeepSeek R1 does not guess; it reasons. And that single distinction changes everything.

The implications of this breakthrough are staggering. The AI revolution is no longer about who can train the largest model with the most data. It is about who can develop AI that actually thinks—that evaluates, corrects itself, and improves with each iteration. DeepSeek R1 marks the beginning of this new frontier. It is the first glimpse into a future where AI is no longer just a tool but a partner in human intelligence, capable of accelerating innovation at an unprecedented pace.

But how did we get here? How did artificial intelligence evolve from simple rule-based systems to complex neural networks capable of independent learning? To understand why DeepSeek R1 is a game-changer, we must first recognize the evolution of AI itself.

For decades, AI development followed a predictable pattern: feed machines massive amounts of data, train them on predefined tasks, and refine their output based on human-provided corrections. The process was labor-intensive, reliant on human expertise, and often limited by the very data it was trained on. While models like GPT-4 demonstrated impressive language abilities, their reasoning skills remained imperfect—prone to errors, inconsistencies, and an over-reliance on memorized patterns rather than true understanding.

Then came a breakthrough: the realization that AI could learn the way humans do. Rather than simply processing data and producing outputs, an AI could be designed to self-correct, reason, and refine its own learning process. This is where DeepSeek R1 excels. It is built upon the principles of reinforcement learning—a method inspired by how humans and animals learn through trial and error.

Picture a child learning to walk. They do not read an instruction manual or memorize a sequence of movements. Instead, they experiment. They take a step, stumble, adjust, and try again. Over time, they optimize their actions, finding the most efficient way to balance and move forward. DeepSeek R1 applies the same principle. It learns not because it is told what to do, but because it figures it out for itself.

This shift in learning methodology has profound consequences. It means DeepSeek R1 is not confined to pre-programmed responses. It means it can solve problems in real time, adjusting its approach dynamically based on new information. It means it can outthink even the most advanced AI models that rely purely on pattern recognition.

And yet, DeepSeek R1's innovations do not stop there. One of its most remarkable features is its ability to perform Chain of Thought reasoning—a technique that mirrors human problem-solving by breaking complex challenges into manageable steps. This is particularly groundbreaking in fields like mathematics, programming, and logical reasoning, where understanding the process is just as important as arriving at the correct answer.

Think about the way an expert mathematician solves an equation. They do not simply arrive at a solution; they show their work, analyzing each step before moving forward. This ability to break down and explain reasoning has long been an Achilles' heel for AI—until now. DeepSeek R1's Chain of Thought approach allows it to navigate complex problems with unprecedented clarity, making its outputs not only more accurate but also more transparent and explainable.

But perhaps the most fascinating aspect of DeepSeek R1's development is the sheer scale of its ambition. The model itself consists of 671 billion parameters, a staggering computational feat that places it among the most powerful AI models ever created. And yet, despite its immense size, the research team has managed to distill its intelligence into smaller, more accessible models. This process, known as model distillation, ensures that the power of DeepSeek R1 is not limited to those with massive computing resources. Even smaller versions of the model—such as the 7-billion parameter variant—have been shown to outperform larger AI systems like GPT-4 in specific reasoning tasks.

What does this mean for the future? It means that AI technology is no longer restricted to the elite few. It means that cutting-edge intelligence can be deployed across industries, from education and healthcare to finance and research. It means that the future of AI is one where intelligence is not just advanced, but accessible.

As we stand at the precipice of this new era, one thing is clear: DeepSeek R1 is not just another AI model. It is the beginning of something greater. It represents a shift from AI as a mere assistant to AI as an independent thinker, a reasoning machine that understands, learns, and evolves in ways that were once thought impossible.

This book is your guide into that world. It is a deep dive into how DeepSeek R1 was built, why it matters, and what it means for the future of artificial intelligence. We will explore the science behind its reasoning capabilities, break down the mechanics of its self-learning process, and examine how it is reshaping our understanding of AI.

Most importantly, we will confront the questions that lie ahead. What does it mean for AI to think? How will models like DeepSeek R1 change our industries, our economies, and our daily lives? And perhaps the most pressing question of all—what happens when AI surpasses human intelligence not just in knowledge, but in reasoning itself?

The answers lie within these pages. Prepare to step into the future.

Chapter 1

The Birth of DeepSeek R1

DeepSeek R1 stands as a monumental leap in artificial intelligence, capturing the imagination of researchers, tech enthusiasts, and industry leaders alike. To fully appreciate the profound impact of this new AI model, one must first understand its origins, the people behind its development, and its role in the rapidly evolving AI landscape.

Who Developed DeepSeek R1?

The DeepSeek R1 model was developed by a team of AI researchers from China, a country that has become increasingly influential in the AI field over recent years. The team's primary goal was to create a model that could compete with, and even surpass, some of the most well-known AI systems in the world, such as OpenAI's GPT models. With the backing of extensive government and corporate investment in AI, as well as access to a wide range of resources, the DeepSeek R1 project was able to evolve at an unprecedented pace.

This model represents China's ambitions to not only lead in AI research but also to establish itself as a dominant force in global technological innovation. The DeepSeek R1 team, consisting of top-tier scientists and engineers, worked tirelessly to build a system capable of not just matching but setting new benchmarks for AI performance. The culmination of their efforts is a model that demonstrates impressive reasoning skills, an ability to learn and adapt in real time, and the potential to revolutionize numerous industries, from healthcare to education to national security.

The Research Team and Their Vision

At the heart of the DeepSeek R1 project lies a dedicated research team, composed of experts in machine learning, natural language processing, and computational mathematics. Their vision was clear: to create an AI model that not only excels in specific tasks but also possesses a level of flexibility and reasoning that could transform industries and everyday life.

Unlike other AI models that rely heavily on predefined parameters and datasets, DeepSeek R1 was designed with a core philosophy of self-improvement. Through its unique reinforcement learning techniques, the model is capable of refining its performance through trial and error, much like how humans learn and adapt. This approach is what truly sets DeepSeek R1 apart, as it allows the AI to evolve dynamically rather than simply being programmed with fixed responses.

The team's ambition went beyond building a model that could handle routine tasks like answering questions or translating languages. They sought to create an AI that could engage in complex problem-solving, demonstrate creativity, and even adapt to unforeseen challenges. This would enable DeepSeek R1 to be applied across a wide range of domains, from scientific research to real-time decision-making in business and beyond.

How DeepSeek R1 Compares to Previous AI Models

What truly sets DeepSeek R1 apart from its predecessors is its ability to reason through problems in a way that mimics human thought processes. Traditional AI models, while powerful, often operate within narrow confines. They are typically trained on vast amounts of data and programmed to identify patterns or match inputs to outputs. However, these models often struggle with tasks that require true understanding, complex analysis, or nuanced responses.

DeepSeek R1, on the other hand, pushes the boundaries of AI by incorporating what is known as Chain of Thought reasoning. This method encourages the AI to explain its reasoning step by step, allowing it to identify and correct mistakes as it works through problems. It is a crucial development because it allows DeepSeek R1 to not only make decisions but also reflect on those decisions, learn from them, and continually improve.

This is in stark contrast to other AI models that, while effective, often struggle with tasks that involve multi-step reasoning or require a deep understanding of context. DeepSeek R1 excels in complex problem-solving scenarios—whether it's solving intricate mathematical problems or interpreting complex natural language queries. Moreover, its reinforcement learning technique allows it to adjust its responses and strategies as it learns from experience, significantly enhancing its accuracy and efficiency over time.

The AI Arms Race: How China is Positioning Itself in AI Development

The emergence of DeepSeek R1 is part of a larger strategy by China to position itself as a leader in artificial intelligence research and development. Over the past few years, China has invested heavily in AI, focusing on building models that can match or exceed the capabilities of those developed in other leading nations, particularly the United States.

The global AI arms race is not just a matter of creating advanced technology—it's about economic power, global influence, and technological dominance. AI has the potential to reshape industries and societies in profound ways, and the country that leads in AI development will likely have a significant edge in various sectors, including defense, healthcare, finance, and even global politics.

China's approach to AI development differs significantly from that of Western nations, especially in terms of government involvement. While companies like Google, Microsoft, and OpenAI are leading AI research in the United States, they operate within a more decentralized system where regulations are still evolving. In contrast, China's government plays a more direct and supportive role in driving AI initiatives, providing funding, infrastructure, and regulatory frameworks to ensure the rapid development and deployment of AI technologies.

DeepSeek R1, as one of the flagship products of this strategic push, signals China's intent to challenge the dominance of established players like OpenAI. By building an AI model that surpasses previous benchmarks in reasoning, learning, and adaptability, DeepSeek R1 could redefine the way the world thinks about AI—and more importantly, the way AI models are developed, deployed, and used.

China's AI ambitions are further bolstered by the country's massive data resources, as well as its focus on talent cultivation in AI fields. With a highly skilled workforce, state-backed initiatives, and a clear long-term vision, China is positioning itself not just to participate in the AI revolution but to lead .

Chapter 2

Understanding DeepSeek R1's Core Capabilities

In this chapter, we explore the core capabilities that distinguish DeepSeek R1 from other AI models, highlighting its exceptional performance in reasoning, coding, and problem-solving. Unlike traditional AI systems that excel in a single domain, DeepSeek R1 integrates multiple learning strategies to handle a wide range of tasks simultaneously. Key to its success is the innovative Chain of Thought reasoning, which enables it to break down complex problems step-by-step, improving transparency and accuracy.

DeepSeek R1 is not only faster and more adaptive than its predecessors, but it also excels in real-world applications across various industries. We'll examine how it benchmarks against OpenAI's models and delve into early tests that showcase its practical potential. The chapter provides insight into how DeepSeek R1's ability to learn independently and scale its performance over time positions it as a game-changer in the AI field, setting the stage for future innovations in artificial intelligence.

What Sets DeepSeek R1 Apart?

The launch of DeepSeek R1 has taken the AI world by storm, not only because of its impressive technical specifications but because of the way it redefines what is possible in artificial intelligence. Unlike earlier models that focused on specific, isolated tasks, DeepSeek R1 integrates multiple capabilities in one coherent system, making it far more versatile and adaptable than its predecessors.

The biggest distinction of DeepSeek R1 lies in its hybrid learning approach. It combines reinforcement learning—a method typically used for developing intelligent systems that can learn and improve based on feedback—with traditional machine learning techniques. This allows the model to build a more comprehensive understanding of various tasks by mimicking how humans learn and adapt to their environment. Where previous models excelled in processing vast amounts of data, DeepSeek R1 excels at learning from its mistakes and adapting in real-time, improving its performance with every task it encounters.

In addition, DeepSeek R1 has incorporated a revolutionary feature: Chain of Thought reasoning. This allows the model to break down problems and explain its steps in real-time, providing transparency in its decision-making process. This technique not only makes DeepSeek R1's reasoning easier to follow but also facilitates corrections when the model encounters an error. The result is a more accurate, reliable, and self-reflective AI.

Furthermore, DeepSeek R1's ability to handle multi-step, abstract problem-solving places it in a class of its own. Many previous models struggle when faced with complex tasks that involve layers of reasoning or decisions based on nuanced data. However, DeepSeek R1 can analyze intricate scenarios, make judgments based on multiple factors, and even adapt its solutions based on the environment or task at hand. These capabilities position it as an AI system that can be applied to a much broader range of industries, from scientific research to customer service to creative fields like art and writing.

What sets DeepSeek R1 apart is not just its innovation in reasoning and learning but also its speed. When compared to traditional AI models, DeepSeek R1 processes information with remarkable efficiency. While its predecessors would take longer to respond to complex queries or solve sophisticated problems, DeepSeek R1 does so in record time, thanks to its advanced architecture and ability to adapt its algorithms as it processes more data.

This combination of flexibility, speed, and deep reasoning powers makes DeepSeek R1 a truly groundbreaking innovation, and one that is poised to transform industries across the globe. Whether it's in solving challenging mathematical equations, writing code, or analyzing real-world problems, DeepSeek R1 has the potential to become a game-changer in artificial intelligence.

Its Performance in Reasoning, Coding, and Problem-Solving

One of the most impressive aspects of DeepSeek R1 is its remarkable performance in reasoning tasks, coding, and problem-solving. These are areas where traditional AI models have often struggled, either because they are too rigid or unable to reason in a way that is adaptable to new challenges. DeepSeek R1, however, excels in all of these domains, marking a significant leap forward in AI capabilities.

In terms of reasoning, DeepSeek R1 utilizes its Chain of Thought method to solve complex problems step by step. This method helps the model to not only arrive at correct answers but also to articulate the reasoning behind them. Take, for example, a mathematical problem. While older models might simply compute the answer, DeepSeek R1 will break down the steps involved, explaining its thought process as it goes. This method is crucial because it not only makes the AI's process more transparent but also allows humans to follow the logic behind its decisions.

The true power of this reasoning technique comes to light in more complicated problem-solving situations. For instance, when tasked with solving multi-step problems or abstract concepts, DeepSeek R1 is able to make connections between pieces of information that may not be immediately obvious. This deep level of reasoning is a critical step forward from the more superficial approaches used by previous models, where connections between concepts might be overlooked or misinterpreted.

In the realm of coding, DeepSeek R1 shows exceptional performance. While AI models have been used to assist in writing code for years, DeepSeek R1 goes beyond simple syntax checking or code generation. By understanding the underlying logic behind different programming languages and frameworks, it can help developers write cleaner, more efficient code. It can even troubleshoot and debug code, finding errors that might be difficult for human developers to spot. This makes DeepSeek R1 an invaluable tool for software development, offering both speed and accuracy that would be nearly impossible for humans to match on their own.

When it comes to problem-solving, DeepSeek R1's ability to adapt and learn from its experiences is what truly sets it apart. As it encounters new types of problems, it doesn't just rely on pre-existing solutions; instead, it experiments, learns from trial and error, and continuously refines its approach to arrive at the most effective solution. This is especially significant in real-world applications, where problems can be messy, unpredictable, and constantly changing.

Whether the challenge is scientific research, healthcare diagnostics, financial modeling, or logistics optimization, DeepSeek R1 has the capacity to tackle complex, dynamic problems with a level of efficiency and adaptability that previous AI systems could only dream of. This multi-faceted capability is one of the key reasons why DeepSeek R1 is seen as a breakthrough in artificial intelligence, offering solutions to some of the most pressing challenges facing industries today.

Benchmarks Against OpenAI's Models

When measuring the performance of DeepSeek R1, it's impossible to ignore the comparisons with other leading AI models, particularly those from OpenAI. The advancements DeepSeek R1 has made in terms of reasoning, learning, and adaptability are clearly evident when compared to the performance of OpenAI's models, such as GPT-3 and GPT-4.

In terms of raw performance, DeepSeek R1 has already shown it can outperform OpenAI's models in certain areas, particularly when it comes to multi-step reasoning and the ability to adjust its responses based on feedback. For instance, while GPT-3 and GPT-4 can perform well in generating text or answering queries, DeepSeek R1's ability to break down complex problems and explain its reasoning process gives it an edge in applications that require deep analytical thinking and transparency.

On several reasoning tasks, such as advanced math problems or nuanced language processing, DeepSeek R1 has demonstrated superior accuracy compared to its counterparts. Its self-reflective learning system allows it to detect and correct errors in real-time, which further contributes to its ability to surpass OpenAI's models in specific tests.

One key area where DeepSeek R1 outshines OpenAI's models is in the adaptability of its reinforcement learning process. While OpenAI's models have been trained on large datasets to generate responses based on probability, DeepSeek R1's reinforcement learning allows it to continuously optimize its performance by learning from its own mistakes and improving its response strategies over time. This process of trial and error, paired with real-time adjustments, gives DeepSeek R1 a more dynamic and flexible approach to problem-solving.

These benchmarks reveal that DeepSeek R1's innovations are not just theoretical—they translate into tangible improvements in real-world tasks. As AI technology continues to evolve, it is likely that DeepSeek R1 will remain at the forefront of this revolution, setting new standards for what AI models can achieve.

Early Tests and Real-World Applications

The true potential of DeepSeek R1 is being realized as early tests demonstrate its capabilities in real-world applications. In a series of trials, the AI model has been applied to industries such as healthcare, finance, and logistics, showing promising results across the board.

In healthcare, for example, DeepSeek R1 has been used to analyze medical data, helping doctors and researchers spot patterns in patient records that would otherwise go unnoticed. It can process vast quantities of information in a fraction of the time it would take a human, providing insights into disease trends, treatment efficacy, and potential breakthroughs in medical research.

In the field of finance, DeepSeek R1 has been used to model market trends and assist with financial forecasting. By analyzing historical data and predicting future movements, it helps financial institutions make more informed decisions, reducing risk and improving profitability.

Real-world tests like these showcase how DeepSeek R1's deep reasoning, adaptability, and ability to process large amounts of data can have a transformative effect on industries. These early applications are only the beginning, as more fields are expected to integrate DeepSeek R1's capabilities to solve complex problems, streamline operations, and drive innovation.

Chapter 3

Chain of Thought Reasoning – How DeepSeek R1 Thinks

In the vast world of artificial intelligence, the ability to think logically and make reasoned decisions is critical to the success of any AI model. One of the groundbreaking features of DeepSeek R1 that sets it apart from other AI systems is its use of Chain of Thought (CoT) reasoning. This unique approach to thinking allows DeepSeek R1 to not only process information but also to break down complex problems step-by-step, just as humans do when confronted with challenges.

Chain of Thought reasoning is not a mere technological advancement but a philosophical shift in how we approach AI development. By enabling DeepSeek R1 to think through problems in a structured, sequential manner, it can arrive at more accurate, logical solutions.

This process is akin to the way humans break down a puzzle or navigate a complex problem in real life. What makes CoT reasoning so revolutionary is that it allows an AI model to generate and refine its own reasoning, rather than simply following pre-programmed instructions.

The power of Chain of Thought reasoning lies in its ability to enhance not just the decision-making capacity of DeepSeek R1, but also its performance in tasks ranging from mathematics and coding to more abstract challenges like decision-making in uncertain or complex environments. By walking through the steps of problem-solving, DeepSeek R1 can improve its accuracy, identify flaws in its reasoning, and adjust its approach as needed. This dynamic process of self-reflection and iteration is what makes DeepSeek R1 such an advanced and powerful AI model.

At the heart of this process is the idea that AI should not just arrive at a solution; it should understand how it arrived at that solution. By explicitly laying out its reasoning, DeepSeek R1 not only enhances its performance but also offers greater transparency. This ability to explain its reasoning is particularly important in fields like medicine, law, and finance, where the accuracy of decisions can have significant consequences.

To understand how Chain of Thought reasoning works in practice, it's useful to look at a few examples of how DeepSeek R1 applies this technique in different domains.

What is Chain of Thought (CoT) reasoning?

Chain of Thought reasoning refers to a method in which an AI system is prompted to break down its problem-solving process into a series of logical steps. Unlike traditional models that provide an answer without showing their work, CoT reasoning encourages the model to articulate each step it takes to reach a conclusion. This technique mimics the natural thought process of humans when tackling a complex issue: we rarely solve problems in a single leap but rather analyze, iterate, and refine our understanding until we arrive at a solution.

For instance, when presented with a mathematical problem, an AI that uses CoT reasoning doesn't simply generate an answer. Instead, it outlines each step—starting with parsing the problem, identifying relevant formulas, applying those formulas, and ultimately calculating the result. This process, though more time-consuming than traditional methods, results in a deeper understanding of the task and ensures that any errors are easier to spot and correct.

How DeepSeek R1 applies step-by-step logic

DeepSeek R1's application of Chain of Thought reasoning is not limited to simple tasks but extends across a wide variety of applications, including coding, problem-solving, and decision-making. When tasked with a complex coding challenge, for example, DeepSeek R1 uses CoT reasoning to break down the problem into manageable pieces. It doesn't just output a solution—it explains the logic behind each line of code, identifies potential pitfalls, and suggests improvements based on its step-by-step analysis.

This approach not only improves the quality of the final output but also makes the AI more adaptable. Instead of being limited to a rigid, pre-programmed set of responses, DeepSeek R1's step-by-step reasoning enables it to flexibly adjust its strategies when faced with new, unforeseen problems. This is crucial for dynamic environments where the AI might encounter data or challenges that were not present during training. By relying on CoT reasoning, DeepSeek R1 can adapt to new scenarios, much like a human might rethink their approach when faced with an unexpected challenge.

The impact of this method is far-reaching. In coding, for example, a minor mistake can have significant repercussions, but with CoT reasoning, DeepSeek R1 can quickly identify errors in its logic and correct them before they cascade into larger problems. This is particularly valuable in high-stakes situations, such as software development, where precision is critical.

Examples of CoT in action (math, coding, decision-making)

To understand the practical application of Chain of Thought reasoning, let's consider a few examples from different fields.

1. Math Problems: Suppose DeepSeek R1 is tasked with solving a complex algebraic equation. Instead of jumping directly to the answer, it follows a series of steps. It first identifies the variables and constants, then applies relevant mathematical principles, such as the distributive property or factoring techniques. As it progresses, DeepSeek R1 evaluates each step, ensuring its logic is sound and adjusting where necessary. This breakdown of the solution process allows not just the final answer but also a transparent path to that answer, which makes it easier to follow and understand.

2. Coding: When given a coding challenge, DeepSeek R1 applies its Chain of Thought reasoning by first analyzing the problem, identifying the key components (such as input

data, desired outputs, and any constraints), and then building a step-by-step solution. For example, when writing a function to sort a list of numbers, DeepSeek R1 might first explain the need for an algorithm like quicksort or merge sort, outline the steps to implement it, and then walk through each part of the code to ensure its efficiency and accuracy. The AI's reasoning process helps identify potential performance bottlenecks and optimize the solution.

3. Decision-Making: DeepSeek R1's Chain of Thought reasoning also proves invaluable in decision-making processes. When confronted with a business or strategic decision, for instance, the AI breaks down the issue by considering various factors, such as risks, benefits, and possible outcomes. It applies a series of logical steps to weigh the pros and cons, exploring different scenarios and potential consequences. The model's ability to reason through complex decisions step-by-step ensures that the resulting choices are well thought out and based on a thorough understanding of the situation.

The impact of structured reasoning in AI performance

The impact of Chain of Thought reasoning on AI performance cannot be overstated. By adding a layer of structure to the decision-making process, DeepSeek R1 is able to produce more accurate, transparent, and reliable results. This structured reasoning process is especially important in fields where accuracy is paramount. In industries like healthcare, law, and finance, AI systems must not only produce correct outcomes but also explain their reasoning in a way that humans can understand and trust.

Structured reasoning also enhances DeepSeek R1's ability to learn and improve over time. With each step of the problem-solving process, the model has the opportunity to reflect, evaluate its logic, and make adjustments. This iterative approach to learning allows DeepSeek R1 to improve its performance continuously, making it more reliable and capable in the long term.

Moreover, the transparency offered by Chain of Thought reasoning is a key factor in building trust in AI systems. In applications where decisions can have life-altering consequences, such as medical diagnoses or legal advice, the ability to understand how the AI arrived at a conclusion is essential. By showing its work step-by-step, DeepSeek R1 provides greater insight into its reasoning process, enabling users to verify and validate its conclusions.

Chapter 4

Reinforcement Learning – How DeepSeek R1 Learns on Its Own

In the rapidly evolving world of artificial intelligence, one of the most fascinating concepts that have emerged is reinforcement learning (RL). It plays a pivotal role in how DeepSeek R1, a breakthrough AI model, learns, adapts, and performs tasks that range from coding to decision-making. Reinforcement learning, unlike traditional methods of machine learning, is based on the idea of learning from interaction with the environment and self-correction. The essence of RL is its ability to improve through feedback, mimicking some aspects of how humans learn through experience. However, what sets DeepSeek R1 apart is the sophistication with which it applies this technique to master complex tasks, making it stand out in the crowded field of AI development.

As we explore how DeepSeek R1 learns on its own, it becomes clear that this model's learning process is not just about digesting vast amounts of data. Instead, it involves a dynamic interaction between the model and its environment. DeepSeek R1 doesn't simply rely on being fed answers. Instead, it experiences a trial-and-error approach, where it continuously refines its strategies through feedback loops, adapting its behavior to maximize performance over time. This process is not only integral to the AI's ability to solve problems but also key to its groundbreaking success in reasoning, coding, and other cognitive tasks.

Reinforcement learning in DeepSeek R1 introduces a new dimension to artificial intelligence, providing it with the ability to not only compute but to make informed, strategic decisions that improve over time. By taking cues from human cognition, this form of learning allows DeepSeek R1 to approach tasks in a highly adaptable and intuitive way, leading to more natural, human-like decision-making. Understanding how this form of learning works and the role it plays in DeepSeek R1's capabilities is crucial for comprehending the transformative potential of this AI.

What makes DeepSeek R1 different from traditional AI training?

Traditional AI models primarily rely on supervised learning, where they are trained on vast amounts of labeled data. In these models, an algorithm learns to make predictions or decisions based on this data, usually with minimal autonomy. However, DeepSeek R1 employs a revolutionary shift with reinforcement learning (RL), which changes how it interacts with data and the world around it. Rather than being programmed with explicit rules, DeepSeek R1 learns by trial and error, similar to how humans learn skills like walking or playing a musical instrument.

The key difference lies in the feedback mechanism that drives the learning process. In traditional AI models, feedback is provided through predefined labels or explicit instructions. For example, a supervised learning model would be trained on a dataset where each example is labeled with the correct answer. In contrast, DeepSeek R1's reinforcement learning framework gives it the ability to explore its environment, make decisions, and receive feedback in the form of rewards or penalties. This feedback helps it improve its future actions, which allows the model to autonomously adjust its strategies and make better decisions.

One of the most remarkable aspects of DeepSeek R1's training process is its ability to learn from experience rather than from a static dataset. As the model interacts with its environment, it builds a mental model of how to navigate challenges, making it far more flexible and capable of handling unforeseen situations. By rewarding successful actions and penalizing unsuccessful ones, DeepSeek R1 gradually fine-tunes its decision-making capabilities. This process leads to improvements in performance, making it much more adaptable than traditional AI systems.

The application of RL in DeepSeek R1 means that the model does not simply perform a task based on preprogrammed knowledge. Instead, it actively engages with the task, learns from its mistakes, and adapts its approach accordingly. This approach mimics the human learning process, where trial and error is a fundamental part of mastering new skills. Whether it is solving a complex mathematical equation or navigating a coding challenge, DeepSeek R1's ability to learn independently and refine its actions over time sets it apart from traditional AI models that rely heavily on external guidance.

The role of reinforcement learning in AI development

Reinforcement learning plays a pivotal role in shaping the development of DeepSeek R1. At its core, RL enables DeepSeek R1 to make decisions based on past experiences and the rewards it receives from those decisions. It's an ongoing process of learning, where the model evaluates each action taken, considering the reward or penalty it receives afterward, which in turn influences its behavior in the future. This continuous feedback loop allows DeepSeek R1 to improve its decision-making over time.

The application of reinforcement learning is critical to achieving a high degree of autonomy in AI systems. With DeepSeek R1, the traditional approach of supervised learning, where an algorithm is merely trained on fixed datasets, has been replaced by an environment in which the AI autonomously explores and learns. By leveraging RL, DeepSeek R1 is able to take a much more active role in its development process. It does not simply regurgitate learned information; instead, it builds a dynamic understanding of its environment, adjusting its actions based on the outcomes it observes.

In practical terms, the impact of reinforcement learning in DeepSeek R1 can be seen across various applications, from language processing to coding and problem-solving. For instance, when tasked with coding a solution to a complex problem, DeepSeek R1 doesn't rely solely on existing code samples. Instead, it learns through interaction—attempting various strategies and adjusting its approach based on the results. This trial-and-error method, while more time-consuming, enables the model to develop a deeper understanding of the task at hand and improve its overall performance.

Moreover, reinforcement learning allows DeepSeek R1 to take on more complex tasks that require long-term planning and adaptation. Tasks like strategic decision-making, real-time problem solving, and even ethical reasoning benefit from the model's ability to adjust its behavior based on ongoing feedback. As the model continues to interact with its environment, its ability to make informed, strategic decisions becomes increasingly refined, leading to better outcomes over time.

Comparing DeepSeek R1's learning process to human

What sets DeepSeek R1 apart from traditional AI models is the way it mimics human cognition through reinforcement learning. While conventional AI models are static and typically rely on labeled data, reinforcement learning enables DeepSeek R1 to evolve much like the human brain. The concept of learning from experience and making decisions based on feedback closely mirrors how humans develop cognitive abilities over time.

In human cognition, we learn by interacting with the world, making decisions, and adjusting our behavior based on the consequences. This trial-and-error process is fundamental to how we acquire new skills and knowledge. Similarly, DeepSeek R1 learns by engaging with its environment, testing various strategies, and refining its actions based on the outcomes of those strategies. Over time, it builds an understanding of how to optimize its actions to achieve the best possible results. Just as humans learn from their successes and failures, DeepSeek R1 applies the same principle in its learning process, making it a powerful model for autonomous decision-making.

DeepSeek R1's reinforcement learning process also mirrors human cognition in its ability to adapt. Humans don't just react to immediate stimuli; they also consider long-term consequences. This capacity for foresight and planning is something that DeepSeek R1 shares. The model is not limited to immediate feedback but is also able to adjust its behavior based on both short-term and long-term outcomes, just like a human would when making complex decisions.

Furthermore, DeepSeek R1's learning process is highly dynamic, much like human cognition. It doesn't simply follow a set of rigid rules but instead evolves and adapts to new challenges. This flexibility allows DeepSeek R1 to handle a wide range of tasks and situations, making it more versatile than traditional AI systems that rely on predefined responses.

How trial and error improves AI decision-making

Trial and error is at the heart of reinforcement learning, and it is essential to how DeepSeek R1 improves its decision-making abilities. In traditional machine learning, a model might be trained to recognize patterns or make predictions based on historical data. While this is effective for many tasks, it lacks the adaptability needed to solve problems that require ongoing learning. Reinforcement learning, on the other hand, empowers DeepSeek R1 to continuously evolve by making mistakes, receiving feedback, and adjusting its behavior based on that feedback.

This process of trial and error allows DeepSeek R1 to learn from both successes and failures, refining its approach over time. For instance, if DeepSeek R1 is tasked with solving a complex coding problem, it may initially make incorrect decisions. However, it learns from these mistakes, adjusting its approach and eventually finding a more efficient solution. Over time, this iterative process leads to improved decision-making and more effective problem-solving capabilities.

The trial-and-error mechanism also ensures that DeepSeek R1 is constantly learning from its experiences. Each failure becomes an opportunity to adjust and improve, leading to a more robust and intelligent system. As DeepSeek R1 interacts with its environment, it gathers valuable insights that help it make better decisions in the future, allowing it to handle increasingly complex tasks with greater efficiency.

Through reinforcement learning, DeepSeek R1 doesn't just follow a set of rules or instructions. It is constantly evolving, learning from its environment, and improving its decision-making process. This ability to learn and adapt through trial and error is what gives DeepSeek R1 its unique ability to excel in a wide range of applications, from coding to decision-making and beyond.

Chapter 6

Policy Optimization – The Science Behind Stability.

In the world of artificial intelligence, one of the core challenges is ensuring stability and efficiency during training. As AI systems grow in complexity, the processes that drive their learning must be carefully designed to prevent undesirable behaviors, such as erratic decision-making or convergence to suboptimal solutions. For DeepSeek R1, a cutting-edge AI model, this is particularly important. Policy optimization plays a crucial role in ensuring that the learning process remains stable and that the system can continuously improve over time without losing control or drifting away from its goals.

Unlike traditional machine learning models, which may focus on optimizing accuracy through simple metrics, DeepSeek R1's learning process involves complex decision-making frameworks, where each action impacts future actions and the overall outcomes. This necessitates a delicate balance: the model must explore new strategies and possibilities while also ensuring that it doesn't deviate too far from what it knows works. The science behind this balance is what we call policy optimization, and understanding its role is key to understanding how DeepSeek R1 learns.

As DeepSeek R1 continues to push the boundaries of AI, its approach to policy optimization incorporates advanced mathematical foundations, as well as innovative techniques to maintain stability. The process of policy optimization is not just about achieving the highest performance at any given time; it's about ensuring that the AI's learning path remains consistent and resilient. This chapter will explore the principles and strategies behind policy optimization, shedding light on the mathematical foundation, the techniques used to maintain stability during training, and why these concepts are so essential to the development of intelligent systems like DeepSeek R1.

The Mathematical Foundation of DeepSeek R1's Training

At the heart of DeepSeek R1's training process lies a set of sophisticated mathematical principles. These form the backbone of the AI's ability to learn, adapt, and optimize its behavior through interaction with its environment. To fully appreciate the importance of policy optimization, it's essential to understand the mathematical framework that underpins it.

Policy optimization is built on the concept of a policy, which is a strategy or set of actions that the AI chooses in response to a particular state of its environment. In simpler terms, it's a mapping from states (or situations) to actions, determining what the model does at each step. The goal of policy optimization is to find the best policy—one that maximizes a particular objective, such as the reward received from the environment. However, this is not as straightforward as simply choosing the action that leads to the highest reward in the short term. Policy optimization must take into account the long-term impact of decisions, ensuring that the model doesn't just optimize for immediate rewards but also builds strategies that lead to sustained success over time.

This is where the concept of value functions comes into play. A value function provides a numerical estimate of the long-term return (reward) expected from each state, helping the model to evaluate the effectiveness of its current policy. By learning these value functions, DeepSeek R1 can determine not just the best immediate action, but also the best overall strategy for achieving long-term success.

Mathematically, policy optimization involves maximizing an objective function, typically a reward signal, that measures the success of the AI's actions. This process involves complex algorithms, including stochastic gradient descent and policy gradients, which allow the AI to adjust its policy incrementally based on feedback from its environment. These algorithms are designed to minimize the error between the predicted value and the actual reward, ensuring that the AI's actions align with the goal of maximizing overall reward.

Another important mathematical concept is Bellman's Equation, which forms the basis for reinforcement learning algorithms. Bellman's equation provides a recursive relationship for value functions, allowing the AI to break down complex decision-making tasks into smaller, more manageable components. By solving these equations, DeepSeek R1 can effectively plan its actions and make decisions that optimize its chances of success.

How Stability is Maintained During Learning

One of the main challenges in AI development is ensuring that the learning process remains stable as the system explores new strategies and adjusts its actions based on feedback. Without stability, an AI model may experience erratic behavior, making it difficult to trust its decision-making or to ensure that it will achieve optimal results over time. In the case of DeepSeek R1, maintaining stability during learning is a top priority, and it relies on several strategies to ensure that the model's development stays on track.

One of the main ways that stability is ensured is through the use of constrained optimization. In policy optimization, the model must continually adjust its behavior based on feedback, but it must do so within certain limits to avoid making drastic, potentially harmful changes. This is where techniques like clipping and K Divergence come into play.

Clipping is a technique used to control the magnitude of policy changes. When the AI receives feedback and adjusts its actions, it's possible that the change in policy could be too large, leading to instability. Clipping ensures that the model's updates are within a reasonable range, preventing it from making sudden, unpredictable shifts. By bounding the amount of change in each step, clipping helps maintain smooth, controlled learning that gradually improves over time.

K Divergence, on the other hand, is a statistical measure that quantifies the difference between two probability distributions. In the context of reinforcement learning, K Divergence is used to measure how much the model's current policy diverges from its previous one. If the divergence is too high, it suggests that the model is straying too far from its previous actions, which could lead to instability. By limiting K Divergence, DeepSeek R1 ensures that its updates are small enough to avoid erratic behavior, while still allowing for meaningful improvements in performance.

These techniques work together to ensure that DeepSeek R1 remains on a stable learning trajectory, even as it explores new possibilities and adapts to changing conditions. The result is a more reliable, predictable AI that can be trusted to perform complex tasks with consistent success.

Techniques like Clipping and K Divergence Explained

As mentioned earlier, clipping and K Divergence are two critical techniques used to maintain stability during the policy optimization process in reinforcement learning. Let's take a deeper look at how these techniques work and why they are so important in the context of DeepSeek R1's training.

Clipping is typically used in proximal policy optimization (PPO) algorithms, which are designed to update the AI's policy in a controlled manner. The idea behind clipping is to prevent large, abrupt changes to the policy that could lead to instability. When an AI system makes a change to its policy, the amount of adjustment is based on the ratio of the current policy's action probabilities to the previous policy's action probabilities. If this ratio exceeds a predefined threshold, the update is clipped, preventing it from becoming too large. This clipping ensures that the learning process remains gradual and stable, preventing the model from overfitting or diverging too quickly.

K Divergence, as a statistical measure, is used to track the difference between two probability distributions: the current policy and the previous policy. In reinforcement learning, the goal is to find an optimal policy, but it's important not to diverge too drastically from the previous policy during updates. By limiting the K Divergence between policies, DeepSeek R1 ensures that its updates are incremental, avoiding the risks of overshooting or underfitting its strategy. This technique helps guide the model towards the most optimal behavior without sacrificing stability.

Both of these techniques play a pivotal role in maintaining a balanced learning process, ensuring that DeepSeek R1 can refine its strategy without losing control. By carefully managing the magnitude of updates and the divergence between policies, these techniques allow the AI to learn efficiently and reliably.

Why Policy Optimization Matters in AI Development

Policy optimization is not just a technicality; it is the very foundation of effective AI development. Without a well-optimized policy, an AI system would struggle to adapt to new situations, make informed decisions, or improve over time. In DeepSeek R1, policy optimization is crucial to its success as an autonomous, adaptable AI model.

By ensuring that the model's actions align with long-term goals and values, policy optimization empowers DeepSeek R1 to solve complex problems, make strategic decisions, and continuously improve. It prevents the model from getting stuck in local optima or making decisions that would lead to poor outcomes. Instead, it enables the model to search for solutions that provide the best possible rewards over time.

Moreover, policy optimization allows DeepSeek R1 to maintain stability and predictability, even as it learns from its environment. This stability is essential for ensuring that the AI can be trusted to perform reliably in a wide range of scenarios, from coding to decision-making and beyond. As DeepSeek R1 continues to evolve, policy optimization will remain a key component of its training process, enabling it to adapt, improve, and perform at its best.

Chapter 7

Model Distillation – Making DeepSeek R1 Accessible

In the rapidly evolving field of artificial intelligence, model distillation has emerged as a crucial technique for enhancing the efficiency and accessibility of large AI models. Essentially, model distillation is a method by which a smaller, more efficient model—referred to as the "student" model—is trained to replicate the behavior of a much larger, pre-trained model known as the "teacher" model. The goal is to capture the knowledge and decision-making patterns of the larger model without requiring the same computational resources.

The concept of distillation borrows its inspiration from the process of distilling liquids:

just as distillation in chemistry involves boiling down a liquid to extract its essential components, model distillation reduces a complex, resource-hungry model into a streamlined version that retains the core capabilities of the original. This process typically involves transferring the "knowledge" of the teacher model to the student model in the form of soft predictions or probabilities that represent the teacher's internal reasoning.

The idea behind model distillation is that smaller models, despite their limited capacity, can still perform impressively well if they are trained to mimic the behavior of larger models. This makes them more accessible, efficient, and practical for real-world applications, especially when computational power or memory is a limiting factor.

For DeepSeek R1, a model that boasts 671 billion parameters, the need for model distillation becomes evident. DeepSeek R1 is an incredibly powerful AI, capable of performing complex tasks like reasoning, decision-making, and problem-solving. However, this immense power comes with a significant trade-off: the model's size and resource demands can make it impractical for deployment in environments where computational resources are constrained. By using model distillation, DeepSeek R1's capabilities can be transferred to a smaller model without sacrificing too much in terms of performance.

Why DeepSeek R1's 671 Billion Parameters Are a Challenge

DeepSeek R1's massive size, with a staggering 671 billion parameters, is a defining feature of its remarkable capabilities. Parameters are the variables within a machine learning model that are adjusted during the training process to improve its predictions. In simpler terms, parameters are like the building blocks that define how a model interprets data and makes decisions.

While the sheer size of DeepSeek R1 gives it a vast ability to learn from data and generate highly sophisticated outputs, this also presents significant challenges, particularly in terms of computational resources, memory requirements, and latency. A model with 671 billion parameters requires enormous amounts of processing power to train, often necessitating the use of specialized hardware like GPUs or TPUs and multiple clusters of machines. Even once trained, such a model demands substantial resources for inference, making it costly and inefficient to deploy in real-world scenarios.

Another challenge posed by such a large model is the time it takes to train. With each parameter requiring adjustment during the learning process, training a model with billions of parameters is a time-intensive task. This long training time not only increases the cost of development but also limits the frequency with which the model can be updated to reflect new data or optimize its performance.

In addition, large models like DeepSeek R1 may suffer from slower inference times. Inference is the process by which a trained model is used to make predictions or generate outputs based on new input data. For DeepSeek R1, the time required to process inputs and produce outputs could be prohibitively long, especially when real-time decision-making is necessary, such as in applications like autonomous vehicles, personalized recommendations, or interactive assistants.

To address these challenges and make DeepSeek R1 more accessible to a broader range of users and applications, model distillation provides a solution. By compressing the knowledge of the full-scale model into a smaller, distilled version, it becomes possible to retain much of the original model's power while drastically reducing the computational overhead.

How Smaller Distilled Models (e.g., 7B) Replicate Its Capabilities

One of the most remarkable aspects of model distillation is the ability of a smaller model to replicate the capabilities of a much larger one.

A distilled model, sometimes referred to as a "compressed" model, has far fewer parameters than the original model but is still able to produce comparable results. For example, a distilled version of DeepSeek R1 with only 7 billion parameters may still exhibit much of the same reasoning, decision-making, and problem-solving abilities as the full 671 billion parameter version.

The distillation process works by training the smaller model to approximate the outputs of the larger model, learning from the teacher model's soft predictions. The key is that the distilled model doesn't need to replicate every single parameter of the teacher model but instead focuses on learning the general patterns and relationships that the larger model has learned. In this way, a distilled model can effectively capture the knowledge encoded in a larger model without needing to replicate its full size.

In the case of DeepSeek R1, the distilled model with 7 billion parameters may still be able to handle complex tasks such as natural language processing, reasoning, and even decision-making, albeit with some trade-offs in performance. While the distilled model may not achieve the same level of precision or sophistication as the full-scale version, it can still provide highly accurate and useful results for many applications, especially those that require fast inference or operate in resource-constrained environments.

The key benefit of using smaller distilled models is that they are much more computationally efficient and can be deployed in a wider range of devices, including mobile phones, edge devices, and IoT systems. They offer a significant reduction in memory and processing requirements while maintaining much of the power of the original AI model. This makes them ideal for applications where real-time responses or low-latency performance is required, such as in conversational AI, recommendation systems, or even autonomous driving.

The Surprising Performance of Distilled Models vs. GPT-4

One of the most interesting developments in the field of AI has been the surprising performance of distilled models, particularly when compared to other advanced models like GPT-4. GPT-4, with its billions of parameters, is known for its high-level capabilities in natural language understanding, generation, and reasoning. However, distilled models, such as the 7B version of DeepSeek R1, have shown that smaller models can still achieve impressive performance, often approaching or even surpassing GPT-4 in certain tasks.

Despite having far fewer parameters, distilled models have been shown to perform exceptionally well in specific areas like natural language processing, text generation, and even decision-making. The reason behind this surprising performance lies in the distillation process itself, which effectively allows the smaller model to "borrow" the expertise of the larger model. While GPT-4 may have more parameters and potentially better overall accuracy, a distilled model can still perform at a level that meets or exceeds expectations in many practical applications, especially when computational efficiency and speed are prioritized.

Distilled models like DeepSeek R1's 7B version have the advantage of being highly optimized for deployment in real-world scenarios. They are faster to train, quicker to run, and require fewer resources than their larger counterparts. This makes them an attractive alternative for developers and businesses looking to implement AI in production environments without the heavy computational burden associated with larger models like GPT-4.

Moreover, the distillation process has shown that smaller models can learn to focus on the most important aspects of a task, often leading to enhanced generalization and robustness. While GPT-4 may struggle with specific edge cases or require more tuning for particular applications, distilled models have the ability to be fine-tuned and optimized for specific use cases, often yielding superior performance in those contexts.

Chapter 8

Real-World Applications and Future Possibilities

DeepSeek R1, with its extraordinary capabilities, holds the potential to revolutionize numerous sectors, driving innovation and enhancing efficiency across industries. Its deep learning algorithms, combined with its massive parameter size and self-learning capabilities, make it an ideal candidate for transforming industries that rely on data-intensive decision-making. Let's explore how DeepSeek R1 can make a difference in healthcare, finance, and education, three fields where the application of advanced AI is not only beneficial but essential for future growth.

In healthcare, DeepSeek R1's potential to revolutionize the field is immense. Its ability to process vast amounts of medical data and generate predictive models can assist doctors in diagnosing diseases with a higher degree of accuracy. For instance, AI models can now detect certain types of cancer earlier than human doctors can, through the analysis of medical images like MRIs and CT scans. DeepSeek R1, with its vast knowledge base, could not only assist in image recognition but also in personalizing patient care by predicting how a patient's condition might evolve based on their medical history, lifestyle choices, and genetic data.

Moreover, in drug discovery, DeepSeek R1's learning algorithms can rapidly sift through existing research and clinical trial data to identify potential therapeutic compounds or treatments. Given the complexity and sheer volume of data involved in modern healthcare, a model like DeepSeek R1 could significantly accelerate the drug development process, helping researchers identify viable drug candidates faster and more cost-effectively than traditional methods. This would ultimately lead to more rapid responses to emerging health crises, such as the COVID-19 pandemic, where speed is paramount in developing vaccines and treatments.

In the finance sector, the impact of DeepSeek R1 is equally significant. The AI's ability to process large sets of financial data could enhance predictive modeling for stock prices, enabling investors to make more informed decisions. DeepSeek R1 could analyze market trends, economic indicators, and news events to predict market movements with a level of precision that human analysts might struggle to match. This capability could lead to more stable financial markets by reducing human error and bias, while also enabling quicker, data-driven decisions for portfolio management.

Additionally, DeepSeek R1 could help financial institutions identify fraudulent activities by analyzing transaction data in real-time. Through deep pattern recognition, the AI could spot unusual transactions or emerging fraud trends that might otherwise go unnoticed. This would not only improve security but also streamline compliance with regulatory standards, making the financial sector more robust and responsive to both opportunity and risk.

In education, the transformative power of DeepSeek R1 lies in its ability to personalize learning experiences for students. Traditional educational models are often one-size-fits-all, but AI systems like DeepSeek R1 could offer highly tailored curriculums based on individual learning styles, strengths, and weaknesses. It could analyze student performance in real-time and adjust the pace or difficulty of lessons to ensure optimal learning outcomes. This would make education more effective, ensuring that every student receives the support they need to thrive.

Furthermore, DeepSeek R1 could help reduce the administrative burden on educators by automating grading and administrative tasks. AI-powered platforms could assess written essays, assignments, and exams with a high degree of accuracy, freeing up time for teachers to focus on more meaningful interactions with their students. For schools in underserved or remote areas, DeepSeek R1 could provide access to high-quality education through virtual learning environments, bridging the gap where resources and qualified teachers are scarce.

In all of these industries, DeepSeek R1's self-learning capabilities would make it not just a tool, but a partner in decision-making, enhancing human capabilities and driving progress at an unprecedented pace.

Ethical Considerations of AI with Self-Learning Capabilities

As AI models like DeepSeek R1 become increasingly sophisticated, the ethical implications of their use cannot be overlooked. While AI has the potential to revolutionize industries and improve human lives, it also raises important questions about how these technologies should be developed, deployed, and regulated.

One of the primary ethical concerns surrounding self-learning AI is the lack of transparency in decision-making. DeepSeek R1, like many deep learning models, functions as a "black box." This means that while it can make highly accurate predictions or decisions, it's often difficult to understand exactly how or why the AI arrived at a particular conclusion. This opacity can be a significant issue in high-stakes areas like healthcare, finance, and law, where understanding the reasoning behind AI decisions is crucial for ensuring fairness and accountability.

In the healthcare industry, for example, AI-driven decisions about patient care need to be explainable to both medical professionals and patients. If a model suggests a particular treatment plan, there must be a clear and understandable rationale for that suggestion, particularly when it comes to life-altering decisions. The inability to explain how the AI arrived at a decision could erode trust in the technology and lead to reluctance in adopting it.

Another ethical concern is the potential for bias in AI systems. AI models, including self-learning systems like DeepSeek R1, are trained on vast datasets, and if these datasets are flawed or unrepresentative, the model can learn and perpetuate biases. In healthcare, for instance, an AI model trained predominantly on data from one demographic group could result in skewed predictions or treatment recommendations that are less accurate for people outside of that group. Similarly, in finance, biased AI models could lead to discriminatory practices in loan approval or risk assessment.

AI bias can also be a significant issue in education, where personalized learning systems might unintentionally reinforce stereotypes or favor certain learning styles over others. Ensuring that AI systems are trained on diverse, representative datasets and that they undergo rigorous testing for fairness is essential to preventing harm and ensuring that AI benefits everyone equally.

Lastly, there are concerns about the impact of AI on employment. As AI systems become more capable of automating tasks traditionally done by humans, there is a risk that jobs in sectors like customer service, education, and even healthcare could be displaced. While AI will likely create new opportunities and augment human work rather than replace it entirely, the transition to an AI-driven economy will require careful planning and consideration of how to support workers who may be displaced by automation.

The Future of AI Competition: OpenAI, DeepSeek, and Beyond

As AI technology continues to evolve, the competition between leading AI developers is intensifying. OpenAI, DeepSeek, and other organizations are all vying to create the most advanced, capable AI systems. This competition is driving rapid advancements in the field, but it also raises important questions about who controls these powerful technologies and how they are used.

OpenAI has been at the forefront of AI development, creating models like GPT-3 and GPT-4 that have set new benchmarks for natural language processing. DeepSeek, with its DeepSeek R1 model, represents a new era in AI, one where self-learning systems with massive parameter sizes are pushing the boundaries of what's possible. The competition between these organizations will likely accelerate the development of even more advanced AI systems, each with its own strengths and weaknesses.

One of the key areas of competition is in the accessibility of these technologies. While OpenAI has made its models available through APIs, the high computational costs associated with running these models can limit their accessibility for smaller companies and individual developers. DeepSeek's approach to model distillation and creating smaller, more efficient models, such as the 7B version of DeepSeek R1, could democratize access to advanced AI capabilities, making them more accessible to a broader range of users.

Looking ahead, the competition between AI developers is likely to lead to even more powerful and efficient models. However, the focus will also shift toward ensuring that these models are ethically aligned and can be used responsibly. This includes addressing issues such as data privacy, AI transparency, and the ethical use of AI in decision-making.

The rise of companies like DeepSeek signals that AI is no longer the domain of a few large players but is becoming increasingly competitive and decentralized. This will likely lead to a more dynamic and diverse AI landscape, where multiple organizations contribute to the development of intelligent systems that can benefit society in diverse ways.

What the Development of DeepSeek R1 Means for AI Accessibility

One of the most profound implications of DeepSeek R1's development is its potential to democratize access to advanced AI. Historically, the development and deployment of large-scale AI systems have been limited to major corporations or research institutions with the necessary resources. The computational costs associated with training and running these models have meant that smaller companies or organizations with limited budgets have been excluded from benefiting from this technology.

DeepSeek R1's innovative approach to model distillation changes that dynamic by allowing smaller models to replicate the capabilities of large-scale systems while requiring fewer computational resources. As a result, DeepSeek R1 could become a tool that empowers a wide range of industries, from startups to small businesses, by providing access to sophisticated AI capabilities that were previously reserved for larger organizations. This shift toward more accessible AI could spur innovation, enabling businesses to create new products and services that leverage advanced AI without requiring massive investment in hardware or infrastructure.

Moreover, the accessibility of AI could lead to more inclusive innovation, where organizations from diverse backgrounds and regions can contribute to the development of AI technology. By lowering the barriers to entry, DeepSeek R1 could foster a more diverse and equitable AI ecosystem, where the benefits of AI are shared more widely and equitably.

Conclusion

DeepSeek R1 marks a groundbreaking leap in the world of artificial intelligence, a model that combines the latest advancements in machine learning with unprecedented scale and capability. It's not just an evolution of the technology—it represents a whole new era. As AI continues to permeate all aspects of modern life, DeepSeek R1's innovations will undoubtedly shape the landscape of AI for years to come. With the introduction of this model, we are witnessing a convergence of technologies that not only push the limits of what artificial intelligence can do but also make these technologies more accessible and transformative across industries.

One of the most profound shifts that DeepSeek R1 enables is the movement from traditional, static forms of AI to self-learning systems that adapt in real-time. With its deep neural networks and ability to process vast datasets at incredible speeds, DeepSeek R1 stands out as a revolutionary force in the AI space. Unlike its predecessors, DeepSeek R1's architecture allows it to go beyond pattern recognition. It is capable of learning from its environment, making decisions based on those learnings, and improving over time. This self-learning ability ensures that DeepSeek R1 is not limited to pre-programmed responses but can tackle new, unforeseen challenges, evolving its understanding with every interaction.

The implications for various industries are vast and transformative. In healthcare, for instance, DeepSeek R1's ability to analyze complex medical data sets could vastly improve diagnostics, drug development, and treatment personalization. By processing everything from medical imaging to patient histories, DeepSeek R1 can provide doctors with more accurate, data-driven insights, potentially saving lives and improving outcomes. Imagine a system that not only recommends the best course of treatment but also learns from new medical research to continually refine those recommendations. This is the power of DeepSeek R1, where AI is more than a tool—it becomes an invaluable partner in driving progress.

In the finance sector, DeepSeek R1 can revolutionize how financial markets are analyzed and decisions are made. Its ability to process vast amounts of data in real-time could provide deeper insights into market trends, enabling more informed investment decisions and helping mitigate risk. For financial institutions, the ability to have an AI that continuously learns and adapts to market conditions means a far more agile, responsive system, one that can predict potential market shifts and advise on optimal strategies. Moreover, DeepSeek R1's efficiency in handling large datasets can assist in combating fraud, detecting anomalies in transaction patterns, and safeguarding financial systems.

Education, too, stands to gain immensely from the capabilities of DeepSeek R1. With its deep understanding of complex subjects, this AI can revolutionize how personalized learning is delivered. By analyzing students' strengths, weaknesses, and learning styles, DeepSeek R1 can create individualized education plans, tailoring content to the needs of each student. Its ability to learn and adapt means that it can continuously improve these plans, offering real-time feedback and adjustments. Moreover,

DeepSeek R1 could assist educators by automating administrative tasks, giving teachers more time to focus on student interaction and fostering creativity in the classroom.

At the same time, the very advances that make DeepSeek R1 a powerful tool also raise concerns about the ethical implications of AI in society. The very idea of a self-learning, highly intelligent machine poses questions about control, bias, and transparency. While DeepSeek R1's ability to adapt and improve itself is an asset, it also highlights the need for ethical frameworks to govern its use. AI systems are only as good as the data they are trained on, and biases in that data can easily translate into biased decisions. Therefore, developing AI models like DeepSeek R1 requires not just technical innovation but a deep commitment to fairness, transparency, and accountability.

The ethical considerations surrounding DeepSeek R1 are not obstacles to progress but important guiding principles. Ensuring that these systems are built with diverse and representative data, as well as a commitment to addressing any biases that may emerge, is essential. Additionally, as AI becomes increasingly integrated into industries that directly impact individuals—such as healthcare, finance, and education—ensuring transparency and accountability will be critical to fostering trust in these technologies. By doing so, DeepSeek R1 and other AI models can serve as powerful allies, helping to solve some of the world's most complex challenges, rather than contributing to harm.

Looking beyond these immediate applications, the true potential of DeepSeek R1 lies in how it will shape the future of AI competition. As AI continues to evolve, it is clear that companies like OpenAI, DeepSeek, and other players will continue to push the boundaries of what is possible. This competition is essential for driving progress in AI development, ensuring that innovation does not stagnate and that new ideas and approaches continue to emerge. While DeepSeek R1's capabilities are impressive, it is likely that the future will bring even more sophisticated models, as research in areas like reinforcement learning, model distillation, and self-supervised learning advances.

The emergence of models like DeepSeek R1 also signals a shift in the way AI is distributed and made accessible to the broader public. One of the most exciting aspects of this technology is how it makes AI more available and applicable to businesses of all sizes. Smaller, distilled versions of DeepSeek R1, for example, offer the same capabilities as the full model but at a fraction of the cost and computational requirements. This democratization of AI means that smaller startups and independent developers now have access to technology that was once limited to major corporations and research labs. As this accessibility continues to grow, we can expect an explosion of innovation in every sector, as businesses and individuals find new ways to leverage the power of AI to solve real-world problems.

DeepSeek R1 represents not just a technical achievement, but a philosophical shift in how we view artificial intelligence. Rather than seeing it as a tool to perform specific tasks, DeepSeek R1 forces us to consider AI as a partner in the creation of knowledge and solutions. It is no longer about simply automating processes or improving efficiency—it is about AI learning, adapting, and growing in ways that mirror human thought and decision-making. This shift has profound implications for the future of technology and society as a whole.

The next frontier for AI will be shaped by models like DeepSeek R1, as they push the boundaries of what is possible while addressing the ethical and practical challenges that come with such transformative technology. As we look forward to the future of AI, it is clear that DeepSeek R1's breakthroughs are just the beginning. In the coming years, we will see even more advanced AI models that continue to redefine the relationship between humans and machines, pushing the limits of what technology can accomplish while ensuring that AI remains a positive force in the world. With the continued evolution of these technologies, there is no telling what the future holds, but one thing is certain: DeepSeek R1's role in shaping that future will be nothing short of revolutionary.

www.ingramcontent.com/pod-product-compliance
Lightning Source LLC
LaVergne TN
LVHW022355060326
832902LV00022B/4466